Exploring Earth and Space

Earth's Water

Desmond Hume

NEW YORK

Published in 2013 by The Rosen Publishing Group, Inc.
29 East 21st Street, New York, NY 10010

Book Design: Michael Harmon

Photo Credits: Cover artcasta/Shutterstock.com; p. 4 kk-artworks/Shutterstock.com; p. 5 (boots) Algecireño/Shutterstock.com; p. 5 (creek) MC_PP/Shutterstock.com; p. 5 (ocean) Losevsky Pavel/Shutterstock.com; p. 5 (pond) Yuriy Kulyk/Shutterstock.com; p. 6 (water) Paul Fleet/Shutterstock.com; p. 6 (grass) J. Helgason/Shutterstock.com; p. 7 Open Hearts Designs/Shutterstock.com; p. 8 Dmitry Naumov/Shutterstock.com; p. 9 zebra0209/Shutterstock.com; p. 10 CAN BALCIOGLU/Shutterstock.com; p. 11 Gregor Kervina/Shutterstock.com; p. 12 2happy/Shutterstock.com; p. 13 Mario7/Shutterstock.com; p. 14 kavram/Shutterstock.com; p. 15 THP Tim Hester Photography/Shutterstock.com; p. 16 Sven Hoppe/Shutterstock.com; p. 17 ethylalkohol/Shutterstock.com; p. 18 Igumnova Irina/Shutterstock.com; p. 19 Stana/Shutterstock.com; p. 22 argus/Shutterstock.com.

Library of Congress Cataloging-in-Publication Data

Hume, Desmond.
Earth's water / Desmond Hume.
    p. cm.— (Exploring Earth and space)
Includes index.
ISBN: 978-1-4488-8818-4 (pbk.)
6-pack ISBN: 978-1-4488-8819-1
ISBN: 978-1-4488-8568-8 (library binding)
1. Hydrologic cycle—Juvenile literature. I. Title.
GB848.H86 2013
551.48—dc23
                                        2012009281

Manufactured in the United States of America

CPSIA Compliance Information: Batch #WS12RC: For further information contact Rosen Publishing, New York, New York at 1-800-237-9932.

Word Count: 375

Contents

The Blue Planet

Earth is sometimes called the blue **planet**. That's because it has so much water! The water makes Earth look blue.

Earth's oceans hold the most water. Some water
is in lakes and rivers. Some water is in ponds
and puddles.

Some water goes into the earth when it rains.

We call this groundwater. Many people dig wells

to reach groundwater.

Some water is in the air. We call this **water vapor**.
The sun heats water on Earth. This causes some of it
to turn into water vapor.

The Water Cycle

The water on Earth doesn't stay in one place. It moves from the earth to the sky. Then it moves back to the earth.

Earth's water does this over and over. It has been doing this for a long time. This is called Earth's water **cycle**.

Water Vapor

The sun heats up the water on Earth. This turns the water into water vapor. Water vapor is like the steam you see when you boil water.

Water from plants also turns into water vapor. The water vapor rises into the sky.

Clouds

Water vapor in the sky cools. This turns it back into tiny drops of water. The tiny drops of water form clouds.

The tiny water drops cling to dust in the clouds. The tiny drops come together to form larger drops. The clouds become bigger and darker.

Rain

The water drops in clouds become heavy. Soon, the water falls back to Earth. This is what happens when it rains.

Rain is an important part of the water cycle. It fills Earth's lakes and rivers. Rain fills Earth's oceans, too.

Groundwater

Some rain **seeps** into the earth and becomes groundwater. Plants use this water to grow. People use groundwater for drinking and washing.

Sometimes the ground can't hold any more water.
Then the water runs downhill. This water forms rivers
and **streams**.

It's Snowing!

Snow is **frozen** rain. It falls from clouds when it's cold outside. The snow piles up on the ground.

Snow **melts** when it gets warmer. The melted snow flows into rivers and streams. Some melted snow seeps into the earth, too.

A Look at the Water Cycle

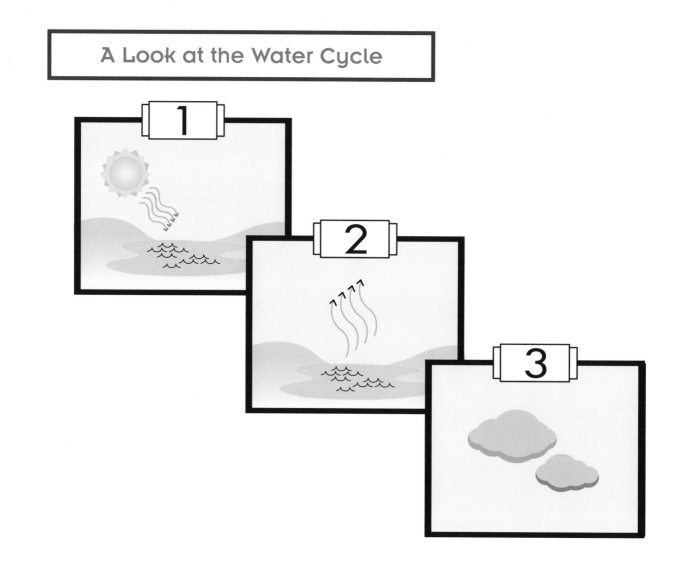

1. The sun heats Earth's water.

2. Water turns into water vapor. It rises into the sky.

3. Water vapor cools and forms clouds.

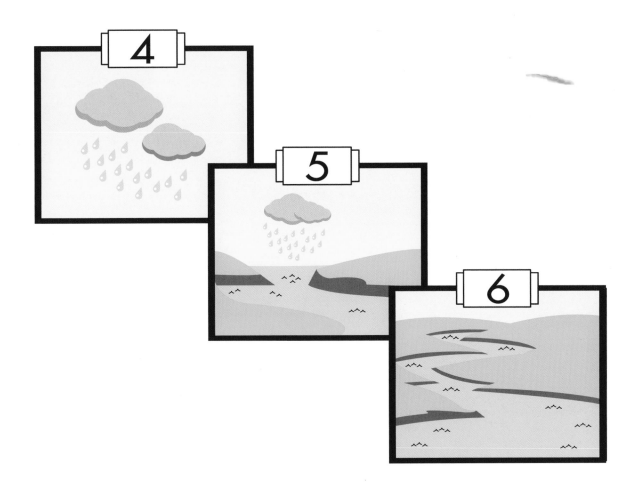

4. Rain falls from clouds.

5. Rain fills Earth's lakes and oceans.

6. Rivers form when the ground can't hold any more water.

The water cycle is important to all life on Earth.

The water on Earth has been here for many years.

It will be here for a long time to come.

Glossary

cycle (SY-kuhl) Something that happens over and over again.

frozen (FROH-zuhn) Changed from water to ice.

melt (MEHLT) To change from ice to water.

planet (PLA-nuht) A large, round object that moves around the sun.

seep (SEEP) To pass slowly into or through something.

stream (STREEM) A small river.

water vapor (WAW-tuhr VAY-puhr) Water in the form of a gas.

Index

Due to the changing nature of Internet links, The Rosen Publishing Group, Inc., has developed an online list of websites related to the subject of this book. This site is updated regularly. Please use this link to access the list: www.powerkidslinks.com/ees/water